Exit Planning:
The Guide for Business Owners

I0471652

Printed in the United States of America

ISBN #: 978-1-257-02479-7

This book is not intended to be a substitute for quality legal, tax, investment, or estate planning advice.

Table of Contents

Introduction

Successfully starting and running a business is a tremendous accomplishment. The purpose of this book is to introduce the types of things a business owner needs to think about before exiting a business, and explore why exiting a business successfully may be even more of a feat than starting and running it.

The field of people looking to exit a business is crowded. This means you are not alone in your quest for a successful exit. Indeed, "the majority of [baby] boomer wealth is held in 12 million privately owned businesses, of which more than 70 percent are expected to change hands in the next 10-15 years," according to Robert Avery, then of Cornell University, and now a Senior Economist of the Federal Reserve Board.

But there's a hitch. The demand for these businesses is not expected to keep pace as the baby boom population wave ebbs. Only the best managed and most successful businesses have the potential to command the attention of buyers and other sources of capital. Among them, only those with solid exit plans will maximize their owner's exit objectives. This is no different than at any other time, except that demographics predict that there are many more business owners today than there are potential owners in the next generation.

The statistics are daunting:

- Some 85 percent of all small business owners do not have an exit plan, a wealth management plan, and/or an advisory team to assist them.

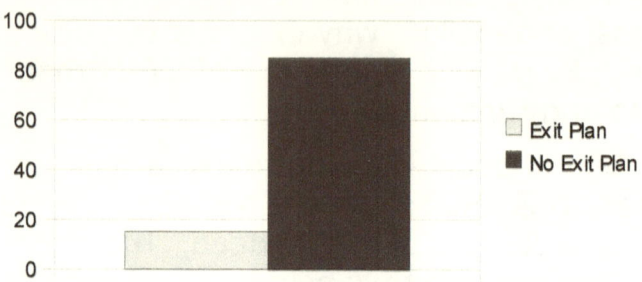

- Twenty percent of businesses with yearly revenues of less than $10 million are for sale, but only one out of four of them actually sells.

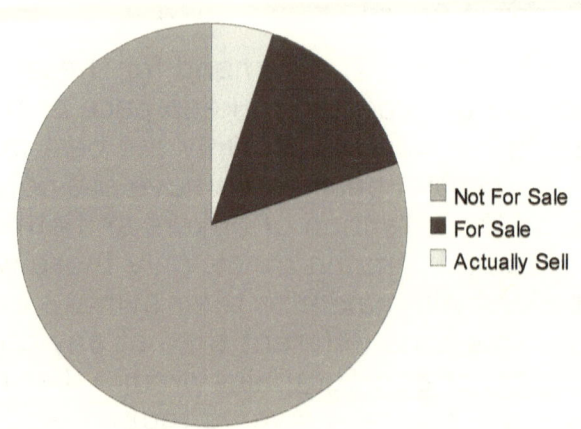

- Businesses with revenues of more than $10 million per year aren't doing much better – only one-third sell (2009, CenterPoint Business Advisors, Lexington, Massachusetts).

So exit planning is crucial. Done well, it sets you up for the greatest return on your investment and makes you one of the success stories – not one of the failures.

In the pages that follow, you will be exposed to the latest thinking about strategic planning for exiting a business, the financial considerations presented by most exit plans, and a description of the personal and human resource challenges most will face in the exit process.

Please read further. At the Vital Growth Consulting Group, we hope this will stimulate you to prepare for the next big step in your journey through the complex world of owning your own business.

Please note: This book was written by three different people – each with a different background and area of expertise. As a result of having three authors, there are also three distinct styles of writing. We anticipate you will notice the difference in styles and now have an explanation for it.

Strategic Planning for Exiting a Business

Start with the "End in Mind"

All good planning starts with the "end in mind". So, your first task as CEO/owner is to list your financial and non-financial goals after the business is no longer part of your life. Now that you've been a successful entrepreneur, what are your expectations and hopes?

Questions to ask yourself:

- Do I have enough money to enjoy the same lifestyle?

- Do I have the means to do even more – travel, philanthropy, help send my grandchildren to college, take up an expensive hobby, etc.?

- Is it important to maintain the family business name or other legacy considerations, such as keeping employment high in the community, maintaining local status, participating on the boards of other businesses and organizations, etc.?

- Do I want to teach and/or mentor others?

- Do I have – do I want to have – enough money to pass on a significant inheritance?

- Do I have the means to care for a variety of dependents? Do I want that responsibility?

- Will I be able to establish targeted gifts and other estate bequests? Is that a high priority?

- Do I want to pass the business on to relatives or other "special" successors?

- Should I sell the business for cash or other consideration?

A gentleman we will refer to as Joseph ran a successful funeral business in the New York City suburbs. He had five sons and three daughters, but despite his best persuasive efforts, not one of them wanted to learn the business. So, nearing 70, he considered selling to a nearby competitor.

Then, when his youngest son heard about that option, the funeral business looked like a good idea after all. The result was a five-year transition plan, including accelerated training and credentialing for the son as well as executive coaching to help develop him as the new owner and face of the business in the community.

In Regard to Financial Goals

Most business CEOs/owners want to at least maintain the lifestyle to which they are accustomed. That means replacing the income produced by a business with income from other sources or income producing assets, or both. The "other sources" might include income from a new business, consulting, board memberships, etc. The income-producing assets might include low risk/low return assets or high risk/high return assets or some mixture of both.

After many years spent building his business, Frank was able to take regular time off and started golfing with his wife. The change from long hours running his business to relaxing with his wife was so enjoyable that

Frank started to think about retirement and life after work.

While exploring what his company might bring in a third party sale, Frank realized it would take a substantial increase in profits for him to walk away with enough to support his desired lifestyle and hope of paying for his grandchildren's college education. Frank was able to reset his expectations for exiting his company but not without significant disappointment and frustration.

With planning and time, you can find a way to provide sufficient financial means to help you achieve reasonable goals. A qualified estate planner can also help reduce your tax burden when assets are distributed (both prior to, and after, death).

When you set those financial goals, keep these considerations in mind:

- How much cash do you need to support your desired lifestyle?

- What are your needs and your dependents' needs? Here we're talking

4

about medical and educational expenses as well as general support.

- Are there any special bequests?

- Can you make a reasonable estimate of your life expectancy, and, where applicable, your dependents' life expectancies?

- Is there a way to minimize your tax burden?

Bill, age 53, planned to retire at age 72, giving him 19 years to accumulate assets. He anticipated living to age 90 and expected to need $150,000 annually to maintain a comfortable lifestyle. He did not expect to make significant bequests or have to pay a lot to dependents. But he did want to avoid estate taxes.

With advice from a retirement specialist and an estate planner, he developed a plan to accumulate the desired level of assets.

In Regard to Non-Financial Goals

Non-financial goals invariably have a financial element, even if it's limited to the opportunity cost of time spent not being paid. So, planning should include having enough income from other sources to pursue non-financial goals. That way, if you want to mentor other business owners (say, as a SCORE counselor), you should have enough money to support that unpaid activity.

Ideally, non-financial goals should take account of:

- The impact of exit timing and financial goals on a plan to pass the business on to a relative or other successor.

- Your desire to take care of long-term employees during and after the sales process.

- Your intention to keep the business in the same community.

- The time needed to prepare for mentoring relationships.

> Larry's business had provided jobs for the community for more than 75

years. Thanks to his grandfather and father, employment held steady through several regional and national recessions. But, having no relative or other successor identified, Larry wanted to find a buyer that was committed to keeping the jobs in the community even though that might reduce the pool of potential buyers.

Ultimately, Larry couldn't find an outside buyer. He was bought out through an ESOP (employee stock ownership plan), which met his goal of maintaining local employment. The financial outcome was satisfactory, albeit less than hoped for.

Current Financial State

The next step in planning is to assess the worth of the business and the CEO/owner – to assess the "current financial state".

Personal Net Worth

The current net worth of the business owner, separate from ownership of the business, is the starting point for calculating how much money must be realized via sale of the business to reach financial goals. While there are countless scenarios, the calculation has five common variables:

- Current value of liquid or near-liquid assets.

- Time before exiting the business.

- Projected value of liquid assets at retirement.

- Non-liquid assets that may be converted to liquid assets before retirement.

- Amount of liquid assets required to sustain a desired life-style.

Of course, the difference between current and required liquid assets must be closed by contributions and appreciation. Ideally, there will be enough time to allow set-aside liquid assets to grow without ill-advised investment risk.

> After selling the business to her daughter, Lisa had a personal net worth of $1.5 million, of which $1 million was in the form of a note from

her daughter, due in five years. The other $500,000 was non-liquid (her primary residence). Her lifestyle was dependent on the interest income from the note and her ability to collect the principal. Given the current economic climate, Lisa is concerned about future collections on the note and has spent many nights wondering about how she might have planned to retire differently.

Henry had run a successful business for 15 years. While he was comfortable from the income produced by the business, he had little in accumulated liquid assets. Considering an exit plan, he realized he would need to accumulate significant liquid or near-liquid assets before selling the business *or* he would have to make a lot of money from the sale itself. Otherwise, he and his wife would have to let go of their accustomed lifestyle.

After consulting with several experts in exit planning, he realized he would require five to seven years to bring in the funds he would need, post sale.

Business Net Worth

The value of the business must also be established or, at least, estimated by a qualified professional. That way you can calculate how much the value must appreciate before a successful exit that meets all your financial goals. A competent business valuation will consider many variables including:

- The nature of the business and its history.

- The general economic condition and outlook of the industry.

- The book value of the stock and the financial condition of the business.

- The earnings capacity.

- The dividend-paying capacity.

- Whether or not the enterprise has goodwill or other intangible value.

- Prior sales of stock and size of the block of stock to be valued.

- The market price of stocks of corporations engaged in the same or similar line of business.

Ultimately, a specific value may be arrived at in one of three ways:

- *Market Approach* – Sales of similar businesses make useful benchmarks. Note that, typically, meaningful data for comparable businesses is very difficult to obtain.

- *Asset Approach* – This generally works for holding companies for investments such as real estate and securities. Overall value is determined by the value of the underlying assets less liabilities.

- *Income Approach* – This applies to businesses that provide goods and services, with value of the entity based on future profits and/or cash flow.

At Vital Growth Consulting Group we have found that the Income Approach is generally the best for exit planning purposes. It considers three factors:

- Benefits that the owner of the business expects to receive.

- Timing of those benefits.

- Risk that the benefits will deviate from expectations.

To estimate value under the Income Approach, analysts use methods such as discounted cash flow (DCF) or capitalization of earnings.

[*Warning: these next couple of paragraphs are by necessity complicated and technical – we've tried to make them as painless as possible.*] Typically, the DCF method is used when growth is expected to fluctuate for several years and then stabilize. That way, future cash flows (or earnings) can be projected for, say, five or ten years. The cash flows (or earnings) for each year are discounted to their present value using a rate that takes into account business risks. For the last year of the projection, the terminal value (value after the forecast period) is often based on capitalization of cash flows (or earnings) using a rate that reflects constant growth (see capitalization of earnings below). That is the discount rate less a long-term growth rate. This value is then discounted to its present value. The sum of the present values of the cash flows for each year (including the terminal value) yields the value of the enterprise before any discounts.

Under the capitalization of earnings method, the expected benefits are divided by a capitalization rate to derive the estimated value of an investment. The capitalization rate includes the consideration of risk as well as growth (of the benefit stream). If the expected growth is zero or constant, then the discounted cash flow and capitalization of earnings (or cash flow) methodologies yield the same value.

To simplify matters, here's a general rule of thumb: the greater the profit – the greater the value!

Before leaving this section, it is worth noting that many CEOs/owners are familiar with EBITDA, or "earnings before interest, taxes, depreciation, and amortization". The formula measures cash flow before consideration of the capital structure – that is, the composition of debt and equity used to finance the business.

But we don't recommend EBITDA for determining cash flow because it doesn't recognize factors such as capital expenditure requirements and non-cash working capital levels.

Consider: Rebecca's business just had its three most profitable years in its 20-year history. But many factors in the industry and the economy gave her pause about her company's ability to sustain those earnings. A large business with substantial resources approached her about acquiring it for more than the value reflected in a recent business valuation.

The clarity she gained from the valuation revealed that she was selling a perceived benefit stream and the risk associated with it. So she sold the business much earlier than anticipated. Two years later the economy started to decline dramatically. The timing of her sale could not have been better.

Closing the Gap between Reality and Goals

Closing the gap between the current reality and both the financial and non-financial goals is the "raison d'être" of exit planning. Put simply, it's a matter of getting from where you are to where you want to be.

Let's start with a rule of thumb: An increase of $100,000 in net profit adds about $500,000 of value. That makes improved operations the shortest route to closing the gap between reality and goals. Upgrading operations begins with a review of the four major decisions driving business growth (based on the work of Verne Harnish of Gazelles, Inc.):

- People – Is the focus on getting the right people and having them doing the right things with clear accountability, metrics and feedback?

- Strategy – Is your top line growing as quickly as you'd like? If not, is there room to improve your strategy and business model?

- Execution – Are your activities logical and logically orchestrated? Are they pursued with discipline? Do they work together and produce the results you are looking for?

- Cash – Cash provides the oxygen for all organizations. Have you focused on cash management and reducing the cash conversion cycle to an optimal level?

To do the review properly, you need a trusted advisor, someone who doesn't work for your firm. That lends perspective that your employees can't offer. A good advisor can tell you about current best practices and point out opportunities you've missed because "that's the way we've always done things around here."

At Vital Growth Consulting Group, we suggest the process begin with a "30,000-foot" review of your business. Components of this review include:

- Key people and management team performance. Are the right people on the bus and in the right seats? Do they work well together?

- Classic SWOT (strengths, weakness, opportunities, threats) analysis.

- In-depth analysis to identify competitive opportunities, threats, and pressures in an industry or market by using a model such as Porters Five Forces.

- Established goals (if any). Are they specific, measurable, attainable, realistic and timely? Does everyone understand them? Are your people accountable for outcomes?

- How long is the Cash Conversion Cycle (CCC) and why is it that long? The CCC covers the time from a sales call or marketing expense, through order entry, production, delivery and billing, ending when money is collected from sale. Decreasing the CCC is a great way to frame the improvement of all important internal processes.

Now you, your team, and your advisor can devise a detailed plan to close the gap. It should include actionable items, specific assignments, and planned reviews. Be sure to lean on your advisor to help with clarity, perspective, and accountability.

Jim's rental business had been in the same location for 30 years and had a good reputation with local contractors and homeowners thanks to outstanding customer service and the variety of equipment for rent. He had a system for retiring equipment as it became difficult to maintain, but the cost of new inventory often made staying current with the latest technology problematic. He was considering reducing the amount of equipment that was made obsolete by new technology and expanding the business to include rental of "party" equipment favored by customers with children – a market with minimal competition. He also hoped that renting "party" equipment would offset the loss of rental income caused by the recent opening of a Home Depot with a rental outlet.

With the help of an advisor, Jim moved out of renting equipment affected by changing technology and into party rental equipment. In the first year after the change, Jim saw a 35 percent jump in overall sales – his biggest historical increase.

The owners of Wholesale Pet Supply had a problem: How to reduce their accounts receivables cycle from over 60 days to less than 28. Their solution: Contact and form a relationship with the accounts payable managers at their top 50 customers. They also began to provide invoice forms as specified by each customer's payable system. Finally, they printed their invoice on blue paper so that it would stand out while being processed by the customer.

The result: The accounts receivables cycle came down to 26 days, realizing a one-time benefit of approximately $500,000 in cash.

The Personal and Human Resource Challenges of the Exit Process

Two of the biggest obstacles to overcome when exiting a business are preparing yourself, and preparing a replacement or replacements. More often than not, successful businesses fail or nearly fail because a CEO/owner struggles to move on or does an inadequate job of preparing a successor. But, if you handle the transition well, this phase of your career can be as satisfying and rewarding as any other accomplishments.

Preparing Yourself

Significant life changes can bring out the best and the worst of people, and exiting a business is no exception. Some leave gracefully while others fight every step of the way, seemingly oblivious to the impact of their resistance.

To exit with grace, you should contemplate what it means to:

- Manage a change in leadership and a period of transition.

- Lose the power, perks, and prestige of leading an organization.

- Plan for the next phase in life, be it a new venture, a hobby, travel, contributing to others through mentoring, volunteer work, etc., or some combination of the above.

Guy ran a construction supply business. He enjoyed it, including his relationships and status with most of his customers. Not wanting to let go of those connections, he did little to prepare a successor or management team to take over for him. Because he failed to plan, he was unable to find a buyer who was interested in acquiring his firm.

Dan had spent much of his adult life building the business his father had started in the 1950s. A health concern prompted him to start thinking about retirement, but without a strong desire to move on from his work, he remained active until ill health forced his hand. Suddenly, time was of the essence and he ended up selling the business to some long-term employees at a fraction of the value he anticipated.

Of all the tasks that go with preparing yourself to exit a successful business, the easiest to underestimate is the highly personal challenge of giving up the power and prestige that go with being a leader. Knowing that a transition is imminent helps, but there's nothing quite like going from the center of power in a profitable business that meets a large payroll, to relative unimportance and insignificance.

Still there is an antidote: A new set of challenges, be they personal or professional. In our experience, those who've charted out the next steps in their lives make the most graceful – and therefore – successful exits.

Preparing a Successor

Identifying

Identifying a successor is often tougher than it may appear at first blush (the exception, of course, being a successor who's related to the outgoing CEO/owner). So discerning the characteristics needed to lead a profitable business, especially through transition at the top, can be a daunting task.

You can start by considering leadership traits:

- Skill and training as, for example, an engineer.

- Training in financial statements and accounting procedures.

- The ability to lead without formal authority.

- The ability to form and lead teams.

- The ability to build positive relationships with key stakeholders.

It is rare to find these traits in a single individual early in a career, but of course they can be developed over time.

Selecting

Once you've identified the skills and personality characteristics needed for the job, you can search for candidates – internal, external, related, or not related. Internal candidates are well known and familiar, if not intimately familiar, with the operation of the business. But they may lack the traits needed to be an effective CEO/owner. They may also have "enemies" within your business who could undermine their authority.

The advantage of external candidates is that they were selected for particular skills and experiences, perhaps including time spent as a CEO/owner. Still, they are unknowns on many levels and they may have difficulty integrating into a business' culture and milieu.

Candidates related to the CEO/owner may or may not have the desired skills and personality characteristics. Success is more likely if the relative has led a business or can develop to the point of leading effectively.

Factors to consider as you select one candidate from a pool include:

- The outcome of any interviews and reviews of relevant experience.

- The results of any assessment tools (personality, motivation, critical thinking ability, etc.).

- A candidate's relationship with key stakeholders both internal and external to the business – ties to other members of the management team, customers, the community, etc.).

Developing

Any plan for developing a selected candidate will have to consider the time before the CEO/owner leaves and the skills, experience, and personality traits desired. Strategies for developing a selected candidate can include:

- Systematic job rotation, particularly into positions with direct Profit & Loss responsibility.

- Focused coaching, based on the results of any assessment tools and interviews and what you expect of your successor.

- Participation in an external forum for executives in similar roles.

Possible Complications

Any plan to identify and develop a successor will have to take into account the possibility of internal resistance and other negative fallout. That may be enough of a problem to delay announcing the appointment.

Vital Growth Consulting Group has found that naming a successor and dealing with any fallout should *happen sooner rather than later.* That way you have more time to intervene and lend your authority to the soon-to-be CEO/owner.

Finally, if you want to sell your business and never look back, then identifying, selecting, and developing a successor may be of little importance to you. But consider: Having a successor ready to take over and held in place by incentives (so called "golden handcuffs") will enhance the value of the business to potential buyers.

Robert's three sons all worked at his company, which manufactured electronic components and had annual sales of more than $100 million. Two of them were key members of the management team and well regarded by peers and subordinates alike. The middle son chronically underperformed and would not have had a job had he not been a family member. Robert's exit plan called for the oldest to be CEO – despite widespread feelings among his employees that he was a gifted engineer and not as talented at managing others as the youngest son. Robert didn't know how to proceed.

After many months of indecision, he sought outside advice. Ultimately, he named his youngest son CEO, his oldest son COO, and gave his middle son a severance package to provide a modest annuity.

Preparing to Sell and Finding a Buyer

In one sense, you have been preparing to sell since you started planning how to close the gap between where your business is now and where you want it to be. In a second sense, preparing to sell takes on new meaning once you have closed the gap. Now the focus turns from improving the business operation to options for selling.

The chief options for a sale are:

- Selling to a third party.

- Selling to the next generation.

- Selling to the current management team.

- Setting up an IPO.

- Selling to all employees as in an ESOP (employee stock ownership plan).

Since data shows that half of companies are sold to a third party, we will cover that possibility in some detail. There are two generic types of third parties:

1) **Strategic buyers** – firms in your industry or complementary industries, or ones that want to enter your industry. In other words,

you have something they want – products, customers, channels, technology, real estate, name, intellectual property, etc. Buying your business brings in revenue, cost efficiencies, talent, and/or time savings.

2) **Financial buyers** – firms and investors looking solely for an acceptable return on their investment.

Strategic buyers are normally preferable because your business is worth more to them than just its current cash flow. In both cases it is standard to "restate" past financial statements for unusual items, such as losses that were incurred in shutting down a non-performing product line the prior year. Or sometimes the current CEO/owner has a number of perks that will go away when the business is sold. These costs should not be considered in the historical Profit & Loss Statements or in future projections when selling the business.

Closing the gap between current reality and goals should include developing detailed information about your particular industry and its trends. With that information and the help of an advisor, you can plan to market your business to a targeted group of potential strategic buyers. Look first for firms that would gain the most by buying your customers, channels, intellectual property, etc. That strategy will typically bring a higher sales price.

After identifying potential buyers, consider one or more approaches to contacting them. For example, you may approach them to form an alliance or you may express interest in a complimentary business unit. Or, you may ask them directly if they want to buy all or part of your business.

Usually, the chief variable in making such a choice is time. It's not uncommon for "courtship" between buyer and seller to take a couple of years, especially for privately held companies. In other circumstances, personal and/or market considerations dictate a much more rapid pace. Each set of circumstances is unique and should be part of the early dialogue between you and your advisor.

At some point, a booklet containing relevant market, product, personal, and financial information should be prepared. The aim of this document is to entice and inform prospective buyers. Done well, the booklet is the vehicle for getting people to the table, ready to sign a letter of intent.

This is the juncture where the seller's team should rigorously perform their own due diligence. Due diligence is a comprehensive analysis of the company aimed at confirming all material facts in regard to a sale. This internal evaluation anticipates the potentially significant issues that would concern a buyer, giving the seller the chance to address problem areas.

Once you develop the plan for selling, you have to execute it. This is where you should decide how much to be involved in the process. Keep in mind that running the business effectively is still paramount. Ultimately, the health and profits of your company will have the biggest impact on sales price.

Most owners only sell one or, at most, two businesses in their careers. As a result, they're not always very good at it. Frequently, they get too wrapped up in the sales process to the detriment of both the business and the sale, for lack of necessary attention.

The other problem with being on the "front line" of selling the company is that it doesn't allow time to objectively consider issues from various points of view. It also removes the "I'll need to ask the owner about that" card from the game.

Finally, the CEO/owner's emotional involvement in the sale cannot be discounted as a crucial factor. Who wouldn't be emotional about selling "my baby?" Be warned: Most strategic buyers have more experience with the situation and use that emotion to their benefit. Once again, an advisor can add value. There is no substitute for multiple experiences selling a business and the ability to remain detached.

Other Considerations of Exit Plans

Exit Team Members

So far, we have described the role of a strategic planner, a business valuation specialist, and an executive advisor. Other specialists who have a role in any competent exit plan include:

- Attorney

- Investment advisor

- Tax advisor

- Accountant

Often these specialists are retained already in support of everyday business operations. If not, or if any of them are unfamiliar with exit planning, you should find a specialist in the field to complete your exit team. At the Vital Growth Consulting Group, we often work with the CEO/owner to lead that effort.

Finally, under many circumstances, it may also be wise to consult with an estate planner, a banker, a financial planner, and an insurance advisor before you're ready to exit.

Death, Disability, Dissolution

It is beyond the scope of this work to describe all the steps a CEO/owner might take to prevent catastrophic fallout from unanticipated death, disability, or dissolution. Still, be aware that the best of exit plans often fail to account for such unforeseen events. Your insurance against the unexpected is to work with experienced advisors from early on in the exit planning process.

Summary

Failure of an exit plan can usually be blamed on the fact that it was given a low priority. Like many things in life, it's not shortage of knowledge or how to do it. Typically the failure can be traced to lack of disciplined execution because the plan never got the attention it deserved.

By now you understand that this document is nothing more than an introduction to exit planning – a means to start thinking about the process. At Vital Growth Consulting Group, we have outlined the essential considerations of solid exit planning. Please consider contacting us for assistance.

Vital Growth Consulting Group

www.vitalgrowthllc.com

155 Fleet Street

Portsmouth, NH 03801

603-766-4926

Bios

Don Sweet, D.B.A.

Dr. Sweet has consistently helped businesses improve their top and bottom line performance. He has 30 years of domestic and international business experience in US and multinational companies, both private and public, in a number of different industries.

Prior to starting his first consulting business in 2000 he held the positions of CEO, COO, and CFO and has had Profit & Loss responsibility for business units in North America and Europe. Don has a Doctor of Business Administration from Nova Southeastern University and an MBA from the University of Connecticut. He has received Executive Education from Dartmouth College, University of Virginia, Northwestern University and Harvard University.

Don can be reached at don.sweet@vitalgrowthllc.com.

Bill Howell, MBA, CPA/ABV/CFF, ASA, CVA

Bill Howell is a seasoned professional with extensive senior management experience and has performed valuations of over 200 companies. His background includes successful performance with two closely held and family-owned businesses performing as CEO (non-family executive) and CFO. He started his career with a Big Four CPA firm in the Boston and Portland, Maine offices.

Bill has an MBA with a concentration in Finance from Boston College and a BSBA in accounting from Bucknell University.

Bill can be reached at bill.howell@vitalgrowthllc.com.

Brad Lebo, Ph.D.

Dr. Lebo has 25-plus years of experience in organizations ranging from small businesses to Fortune 100 firms. He is an expert at enhancing performance through effective assessment and targeted individual development. His areas of specialization include executive role development, managing complex business relationships (including family situations), leadership development, team process improvement, increasing individual influence, and individual and team emotional intelligence.

Brad holds a Ph.D. in Counseling Psychology from Northeastern University, a Masters Degree in Industrial Counseling from

Northeastern University, and a Bachelors
Degree in Economics from Colgate University.

Brad can be reached at
brad.lebo@vitalgrowthllc.com.

Appendix – Sale Examples

How Businesses Have Been Sold

SOME DETAILS HAVE BEEN CHANGED TO PROTECT CONFIDENTIALITY.

Example 1 – small business with issues on transferability of the revenue stream

- Small consulting firm with two partners – annual revenues of approximately $500,000.

- One wanted to stay and the other wanted to leave for an opportunity with a client.

- The practice had been very successful since inception five years earlier, but the economy was starting to slowdown and revenues from a significant client were expected to decline.

- Sales were largely dependent on relationships with a network of professional referral sources developed by the departing partner.

- There was basically nothing to transfer except the net assets of the firm.

- After subtracting for estimated overhead costs over the next few months, the net assets were allocated between the owners on a pro-rata basis.
- The partner who wanted to stay continued to run the firm as a sole owner.

Example 2 – sale to a much larger business

- The company and the buyer were both involved in the manufacturing and distribution of specialty medical devices. The company's annual revenues were around $25 million – although growing quickly.
- The CEOs of each business knew each other from trade association meetings and conventions.
- An offer was made based on a multiple of EBITDA (earnings before interest, taxes, depreciation, and amortization).
- Examples of terms that could apply to such an acquisition in the current market:
  - Consideration in the forms of cash and an earn-out under a specified formula (contingent consideration based on

the achievement of specified performance or objectives).

- Provisions in an earn-out might include:
  - Defined time-frame of one to four years during which succession management can be developed.

  - Additional consideration based on a formula tied to the achievement of specified levels of EBITDA and sales over the earn-out period.

  - Provisions to mitigate the risk of sandbagging the achievement of growth, such as using multiple metrics (i.e., growth in gross margin dollars and EBITDA), requiring EBITDA to increase each year, etc.

- One of the risks of formulas is that they can be rigid and not adequate for addressing changing circumstances. For example, what if the company is restructured during the earn-out period with other affiliated businesses – or an acquisition opportunity arises. The point is that the formula may need to be revisited.

Example 3 – distressed business

- Manufacturer of prominent brand name athletic clothing products was in bankruptcy and acquired by investors for a nominal cost. Annual revenues were approximately $10 million.

- While the bankruptcy was helpful for shedding obligations, the business required a turn-around in order to be viable.

- Significant capital investments were required to fund operating losses and working capital requirements in order to make the business viable.

- The investors were able to sell the company in one year to a much larger business that was formed to purchase companies with strong brands around the country.

- The price was a negotiated amount that resulted in a return that was acceptable to the investors. The buyer was very sophisticated and felt the strategic value of the brand name justified the acquisition cost.

- The ongoing role of the sellers was limited to less than 30 days.

Example 4 – typical for a private equity group deal

- A business person wanted to acquire a food products manufacturing business with approximately $75 million in revenues.

- Financing would require private equity capital and bank debt.

- The capital from the debt and equity available to him was consistent with a recent article by Rob Slee on Middle-Market M&A with reference to a study by Pepperdine University on private equity capital groups:

  o The typical private equity group deal in the current market is as follows:

    ▪ 48% equity

    ▪ 52% debt

    ▪ The debt is based on 2.5 times historical EBITDA.

    ▪ A 2.5 times EBITDA for debt with a 48%/52% capital structure results in an acquisition multiple of 4.8 times EBITDA.

- The 4.8 is less than the general range of 5 to 6 that many businesses aspire to.

Example 5 – typical for a family business with an intergenerational transfer

- The company was a wholesale distributor of hardware products with revenues in the $50 million range.

- The majority shareholder wanted to sell the company and retire.

- The owner's son had a 25% interest in the business in the form of non-voting common stock. More importantly, he really wanted to own the entire company.

- A non-family executive was running the business and did not want to purchase it. Further, he wanted to leave within the next two years.

- A transaction was structured for the owner's son to purchase the business. The services of the non-family executive were retained for another year, with an incentive in place to help ensure that he stayed.

- The purchase price was based on an estimate of fair market value under terms that were agreeable between the buyer and seller.

- Because the acquisition required bank funding, the terms needed to be acceptable to the lender.

- Without getting into the specifics of that transaction, a general structure would apply to today's market – based on a recent discussion with a banker:

  o Typically – without real estate

    ▪ 10% to 20% of cash from buyer

    ▪ 10% to 20% of price from note with seller (i.e., the current owner who is selling the business)

    ▪ Bank finances 60% to 80% - assuming that the cash flow adequately supports the requisite payments under the bank note.

    ▪ Best case scenario which assumes stable history of cash flow, solid future expectations, strong management team, and good collateral for the loan – 10% down and 90% with an SBA loan

  o As for owner-occupied real estate, there are currently very attractive financing programs. For example, sample terms include 10% equity, 50% bank debt, and 40% through the SBA with 20 year fixed rates in the 5% range on the SBA portion.

Example 6 – $70 million industrial components business sold to $250 million competitor

- Business had production and distribution facilities in three countries.

- Commodity business, hard to differentiate from competitors.

- Distribution primary channel to the market.

- 7 Billion dollar industry.

- Industry dominated by 3 large competitors.

- Needed to grow or sell, tried to buy competitors, entered into discussions with prospects.

- One prospect/competitor offered to buy at the right EBITDA multiple.

- Contract given to key personnel to stay with the business.

- Business was sold as an asset sale including all real estate for cash.

Example 7 – 50+ year mfg with $7 million sales in world wide health care market

- 50+ shareholders in total but voting control within a group of 5 shareholders.

- Business needed additional capital to continue investment in R & D.

- Direct selling to customer was usual channel to the market.

- Industry had been consolidating and reducing the company's customer base.

- Larger customers driving down prices and margins.

- Technology continued to advance and company struggled to keep up.

- Looked for strategic partner to enter into joint development or a joint venture as a way to enter into dialogue with prospects.

- Found public company in marketplace that was not direct competitor that wanted to expand market presence.

- Developed two other prospects to provide competition and quasi auction situation.

- Entered into LOI with first company and secured earnest money non-refundable deposit to take the company "off the market" and open negotiations.

- Six month negotiations ending in asset deal for cash that did not include real estate.

- Signed long term lease for buildings with business buyer.

- Had to provide 18 month decreasing escrow to buyer for potential liabilities.

- Began marketing property separately. Needed Phase II DEP work on ground contamination to clear for sale.

- Sold real estate to investor needing a 1031 exchange (a type of real estate transaction permitted under the Internal Revenue Code under which no taxes are owed).